I thoroughly enjoyed reading this work. The pandemic has continued to force us to make changes in the way we navigate the world. It has reshaped educational delivery, our daily routines, and our methods of interacting with each other. Dr. Walker shares content information with opportunities for self-reflection. It is the inclusion of self-reflection that moves us to positivity. Bravo for providing a space for this dive into self-awareness!

- Denine A. Goolsby, M.Ed.
CREATE for Education board member and contributing author SEL Worldwide advisor and professional development facilitator

A must-read for teachers—indeed, all educators—who struggled during the pandemic and who are challenged to find normalcy in a post-pandemic world. The author explains the emotions that contribute to being stuck in the pain of the pandemic, then provides a practical guide to change perspectives and behaviors to find a new normal. This easy read will help you understand the impact of the pandemic and assist in pivoting toward new growth to attain a new level of personal and professional peace.

- William J Zelei, MBA, Ed.D.

TEACHERS OF THE PANDEMIC

From Resilience to Recovery

Dr. Andrea C. Walker

Halo
PUBLISHING
INTERNATIONAL

The views and opinions expressed in this book are those
of the author and do not necessarily reflect the official
policy or position of Halo Publishing International. Any
content provided by our authors are of their opinion
and are not intended to malign any religion, ethnic
group, club, organization, company,
individual or anyone or anything.

ISBN: 978-1-63765-201-5
LCCN: 2022903901

Halo Publishing International, LLC
www.halopublishing.com

Printed and bound in the United States of America

To all employees in schools who pulled off
the near-impossible to make teaching and
learning possible during the pandemic.

To the health-care workers, to
whom we owe our gratitude.

To the essential employees who
kept the world running.

To my parents, thank you for
everything. I love you.

To my daughter, who taught
me the most about life.

To God, thanks for knowing the plans for my
life. I'm grateful Your thoughts toward me are
always good and that I prosper in all areas.

"For I know the plans I have for you," declares
the Lord, "plans to prosper you and not to harm
you, plans to give you hope and a future."

Jer. 29:11

Contents

Introduction

Education Profession x Pandemic Deficit = Employee Burnout

For most of us, being an educator comes with the love of our students, the profession, and our colleagues. Every lesson created generally has an element of care that most outside of the field of education will never understand. Teaching in and of itself is a strategy! It's like a big game of chess. For those who are unfamiliar with the game of chess, to win the game, you must capture your opponent's king, or complete a move called a checkmate. A checkmate occurs when your opponent cannot move his king to another square, protect it by another piece, or capture the checking piece. The game is considered drawn when no one has a legal move to make. It's the worse position to be in because no one wins, and with no declared winner, both opponents feel as if they've lost, or as if the best strategy to win is still obscurely out of reach. Essentially, education is one of the biggest professional games of chess I have ever known. Our profession has conformed to new or encroaching rules or mandates, and often we have been able to avoid being checkmated. However, when the pandemic hit, many of us felt we were at a stalemate. We found ourselves with limited to no moves and have been in a state of stalemate for the last few years.

In education, I feel the ultimate loss occurs when educators as a whole stop doing or fighting for what is best for kids. Throughout the pandemic, most of us didn't stop fighting. In fact, we fought so hard we feel an overwhelming sense of emotional exhaustion that continues to cripple our field.

Have you ever watched a child have a total meltdown? A full-fledged emotional break, with crying and deep, uncontrollable hyperventilating and heaving? Often at some point, that child falls asleep, and upon awakening, the world seems clearer, the problem does not seem as large, and the negative feelings dissipate. Educators around the world are in or have been in a state of a total meltdown, but unfortunately, they have not had the benefit of "going to sleep" to clear their minds. Many are still heaving. For almost two years, there has been a deep, heavy cry made by educators, with no relief.

Those in education—superintendents, teachers, secretaries, bus drivers, classroom aides, lunch staff, and more–have felt the pressures of every intricate nuisance the pandemic has presented in a way that's indescribable. Finally, we are beginning to see some (hopefully) long-term relief that the education profession can reclaim.

The pandemic was more than "just" one event. The emotions that educators feel are valid, and a mishmash of what has happened over the past few years, the present-day pain, the uncertainty of the future, and the individual interpretations of what the pandemic has meant to all of us. This book is for those who have had all ten fingers and all ten toes on the ground in the field of education. For those who taught virtually and in-person. For the thousands who left the profession because of the intensity of the overwhelm. This book goes beyond self-care and resilience. It touches on something much deeper. This book will serve as a segue into our collective recovery. We will take a mental, emotional, and physical journey together. Nothing may completely absolve the fragility of the human experience during the pandemic, but in our resolution to move forward, we will discover strategies and exercises to help release ourselves from the grip of the pandemic. Recognizing your personal power, nurturing yourself, changing your thoughts, and discovering how to manage your feelings, all while actively recovering, will all be a part of this journey.

Chapter 1

Betrayal: The Emotional Pain of the Pandemic

Have you ever looked at the pandemic as a betrayal? The pandemic betrayed the routine nature of our lives and what we knew as "normal" to the point that we are not certain if or when we will get back to what we used to know. As we continue to muddle on in the pandemic, we are realizing that much of our grief is about the loss of normalcy. The pandemic has riddled us with different types of death, insecurity, and insurmountable challenges. The betrayal of the pandemic awakened a pain and an unrelenting exhaustion that we never knew existed.

Do you remember the events of the pandemic that triggered your emotions? What is still adding to the hurt, confusion, and/or change you are experiencing now? The pandemic's role in the life of an educator has made an imprint, and all the feelings of this experience are stored in your body. Your emotions don't care about the actual pandemic. Believe it or not, your emotions only recognize the pain of the pandemic—the pain of what was or what was awakened and rose up.

Like a tangled chain with burrs, the pain of the pandemic wove itself into every emotion you ever felt. Pain is combined with joy. Pain is combined with grief. Pain became present with every emotion we can imagine. That, my friends, has been the weight of the pandemic, this unending heaviness of it all.

It's the love and the loss of the profession of teaching. It's the joy and the loss of the relationships with your students and staff. It's all the things in our personal lives too. It's the love of a spouse but the pain of a pending divorce. It's the hope of recovery but the pain of death. The lifting of mask mandates to the reinstituting of the mandates.

The constant ebb and flow creates instability. Instability for anyone makes it difficult to move forward confidently. We don't want to move too far from disappointment lest we miscarry hope again. It's like we've somehow conditioned ourselves to wait for the other shoe to drop. Not trusting ourselves, and each additional consequence of the pandemic, complicates the feelings involved. No wonder moving forward can be so difficult.

Although far from perfect, comparatively, life seemed a bit easier before the pandemic. Literally overnight, everything we thought we knew about the education profession, even ourselves as professionals, changed on a dime.

The shattering of the old systems hasn't all been bad but sorting through all the changes meant learning the truth about ourselves and about the educational system. These truths are somewhat challenging, but they will lead us to discover some wonderful and delightful things. You may feel as if you are on unstable ground as you get to know yourself again.

It takes strength and courage to uncover the person you think you lost and the profession you had to reimagine. That strength and courage is within, just waiting to be rediscovered. The push to rediscover our fit in education, especially when what has defined us is no longer the same, will be deep and complex. We will discuss strategies to resolve these feelings in detail later in the book, but for now, turn the page and commit your thoughts to paper. The following questions will help you to complete your first journal entry.

Teachers of the Pandemic
Journal Entry

Chapter 1

List at least five feelings you have about the pain you are feeling. List more if you can. Write about how you've changed from before the pandemic occurred until now. How have your dreams for the future changed? Do you have any doubts about yourself? Doubts about the education profession? If so, please list them here.

_____

_____

_____

_____

_____

_____

_____

_____

_____

_____

_____

_____

_____

_____

_____

_____

_____

_____

_____

_____

_____

_____

_____

Teachers of the Pandemic

Chapter 1 Affirmations

I am allowed to cry. These past few years have been hard,

I know that crying can be good for me. I give myself permission to let my tears fall.

Crying relieves my stress. *My tears help to wash toxins and stress hormones out of my body.* I feel cleansed and refreshed.

Crying shows me where I want to make changes in my life. I look for the reasons behind my anger and sadness. I work at becoming more assertive or dealing with rejection. I find more constructive ways to handle situations that disturb me.

Crying gives me the opportunity to see that others care about me. *My relationships grow stronger when I allow myself to be vulnerable and accept assistance from others.*

Crying reminds me to treat myself gently. My life is precious, and my well-being is important. I accomplish more when I respect my limits and pay attention to my needs.

Once I find an appropriate time and place, I cry for as long as I need to. Then I pick myself up and work on finding solutions. *Instead of wallowing in my sorrows, I turn my tears into a healing force.*

Today, I allow myself to have a good cry if I feel like it. I regard my tears as my friends. When I accept my feelings, I can put them in perspective and move on.

Chapter 2

Ouch, This Hurts!: The Physical Pain of the Pandemic

The emotional pain of the pandemic has a physical cause, and having difficulty releasing it isn't a weakness of character. Not only do emotions from similar past wounds combine with newer feelings from the pandemic, but our body also produces chemical reactions that make our recovery difficult. Emotions trigger parts of our brain, and the body's stress response causes physical pain along with the emotional distress you are already feeling.

Our brains and bodies reacted immediately to the pandemic. The brain is so intricately detailed, and our emotional responses to an event as big as the pandemic were and continue to be instinctive. Not only that, but our bodies developed physical responses to help us stay alive. This makes it difficult to release the painful feelings. Your brain activates a series of physical responses resulting in chemical production that affects your thoughts and feelings. Your limbic, or emotional, brain reacts to emotional pain. This can activate the stress response, producing fear and anxiety.

Prolonged or extreme emotional trauma can result in PTSD (post-traumatic stress disorder). PTSD can cause changes to the brain that can be long-lasting. The result is extreme emotional sensitivity that affects your relationships with others, with yourself, and with your school environment. In addition, when the prefrontal cortex, the thinking part of your brain, is stressed, it becomes difficult to think clearly and may cause problems with your memory. Physically, the stress response, also called the fight-flight-freeze response, activates stress hormones.

Adrenaline is produced by your adrenal glands, which rest on top your kidneys. Adrenaline focuses your attention on painful experiences. This focus makes recovery difficult. Norepinephrine, produced by the adrenal glands and the brain, is similar to adrenaline. Norepinephrine when combined with adrenaline is designed to help you run away in a stressful situation or fight to save your life. The challenge with the emotional toll of the pandemic is that there is no place to run, so you end up "stewing in your own juices." Cortisol, activated by the brain and produced by the adrenal glands, is the stress hormone that does the most damage. It weakens your immune system, can disturb your digestive system, and cause weight gain, otherwise known as "pandemic pounds."

Stress hormones can save your life when you need to react immediately, for example if you need to jump out of the path of a speeding car, but when it comes to the emotional punch of the pandemic, stress hormones can interfere with your health. They affect your sex hormones, increasing estrogen in both men and women, which will make you more sensitive to stress. Since women have more estrogen to begin with, this affects women more. Higher estrogen levels in both men and women leads to an increase in depression. Does any of this sound familiar? Do things make a bit more sense?

The following questions will help you complete your second journal entry. For each question, consider how you have changed while teaching during the pandemic.

Teachers of the Pandemic
Journal Entry
Chapter 2

Evaluate how much the following emotions have changed for you on a scale of 1 to 5.

1. Not at all

2. About 25% more

3. About 50% more

4. About 75% more

5. 100% or more than before the pandemic

Anxiety: _____

Affirmation to say aloud: Anxiety was chemically created by my body, and I will be able to reduce it.*

Depression: _____

Affirmation to say aloud: Depression was chemically created by my body, and I will be able to reduce it.*

Hopelessness: _____

Affirmation to say aloud: Hopelessness was chemically created by my body, and I will be able to reduce it.*

Mental Confusion: _____

Affirmation to say aloud: Mental confusion was chemically created by my body, and I will be able to reduce it.*

*For those who suffer from the aforementioned diagnoses, this is not to downplay serious medical conditions. I suffer from anxiety and know the struggle of managing my daily care pre-pandemic. During the pandemic and as we hopefully go into post-pandemic times, there seems to have been a great increase in both student and staff with new mental health diagnoses. I take great lengths to manage my care. If you are struggling, please take solace in three things: You are not alone or weak; help is available; and things can get better. For those who need more help, find a health care provider to diagnose, support, and treat your specific needs.

Teachers of the Pandemic

Chapter 2 Affirmations

I give myself room to grow and heal from the pandemic.

I validate my feelings, but I allow myself to move beyond the memories.

I understand it takes time to heal from the pandemic. I accept that my past experiences during the pandemic are a part of my being, but also that they are from events in the past. I can avoid letting them affect my present and my future.

I clear my mind of negative emotions left over from the pandemic. I forgive past injustices and those who hurt me. I meditate, pray, and even exercise to rid my body and mind of any stress.

My spirit remains strong, despite the pandemic.

I am integrated with the ebb and flow of the universe. I accept that life brings both positive and negative experiences. This acceptance enables me to grow.

Whether I am enjoying good times or if life is less than ecstatic, I find the benefit from each experience. I make cherished memories in the good times. I learn life lessons and gain wisdom in both pleasant and troubling times.

Today, I am safe and whole.

I have inner balance. I recognize my ability to overcome the past, and I look forward to a bright future.

Chapter 3

The Power of Thoughts

Now that we understand more about the emotional and physical responses of our body to the pandemic, let's look at how we've all processed the information we have received.

It is a natural attempt to want to make sense of the pandemic. Unconsciously, we cycle through many questions, such as: Why? What? And how?

It's crucial to realize our thoughts are so powerful that they can intensify our emotional pain by increasing the production of the chemicals and hormones we discussed in the last chapter. The pandemic has done enough; try not to make the pain worse by remaining in your own thoughts. Instead, bring healing to yourself through your thoughts. Recognize the areas that are sabotaging your healing and discover how to stop them by seeing if the following applies to you:

You keep thinking about what happened. When you're caught up in the emotions and memories of the pandemic, your subconscious mind responds as it did when the pandemic first occurred in March 2020. It produces the same stress hormones, creates the same neurotransmitters, and makes the same tracings in your brain.

- **Continuing to recall hurtful areas of the pandemic re-injures your brain.** Your brain and body respond just as they did when it first happened. Instead of being betrayed once, you are betrayed as often as you relive what happened.

- **Find something wonderful and marvelous to think about** instead of reviewing the painful pandemic in the past . Remind yourself of the good that still exists.

Stick to the facts of the pandemic. This is not a political post. In the simplest form, when we fill gaps with inference or inflection about what has happened, we are also creating feelings. And our feelings have our bodies producing all the chemicals. Which then has us feeling worse. Which has our bodies creating more chemicals, which... I think you get my point! Stop the cycle!

- **It's common for us to try to make sense of what is happening, but if you didn't see it or hear it directly, precede your interpretation of the events with "the story I'm making up is..."** This helps you to realize that you may not know everything, and that what you believe could potentially not be true.

Certain friends and family keep you stirred up. Our friends and family hopefully want to support us; however, some may have been terribly impacted by the pandemic. Those who get their negative feelings stirred up continue to help **you** relive negative events again. Reread that. They need to heal, and you need to heal. Unapologetically, set hard and soft boundaries. This can look like the following:

- **Saying no without an explanation.**

- **Turning your phone off.**

- **Practice responses to accepting help from the right people.**

Your self-talk can support your healing or make it more difficult. Avoiding reliving painful situations by putting boundaries in place. By managing your thoughts, you'll decrease the chemicals in your body, which affects your attitude and mood. These strategies will assist you in breaking the habit of continuing to live in the pandemic. Once you quit thinking about it, you can move back into happiness.

In the next chapter, you'll explore the concept of forgiveness: what it is and what it isn't. Before moving on, please anchor in this lesson by spending a few minutes answering the following reflection questions.

Teachers of the Pandemic
Journal Entry
Chapter 3

The following questions are designed to assist you in getting to know yourself better. Answer them as fully as you can.

1. Think back to how teaching in the pandemic hurt you emotionally. How often did you keep reliving the situation? What did reliving the situation do to you and for you?

_____

_____

_____

_____

_____

_____

2. What kinds of stories did you make up about what happened? Explore the motives you attached to the situation and what you inferred as your thoughts about yourself.

_____

_____

_____

_____

_____

_____

3. Consider a time when the support of family, colleagues, or friends kept the pain of the pandemic alive. Explore how their bringing up the pandemic either helped you or hurt you.

_____

_____

_____

_____

_____

_____

Teachers of the Pandemic

Chapter 3 Affirmations

I can control my thoughts.

I take direct action to manage my thoughts. An important part of controlling my mind is the ability to stop any unwanted thoughts. When I experience the same idea repetitively, I make a conscious decision to limit how long I will think about that topic. This way, I prevent my thoughts from tiring me emotionally.

Although any challenging event can trigger me to have recurring or troublesome thoughts, I usually manage my mind well. Calmly, I reflect on whatever the situation is that I am experiencing. My deliberations are focused.

I resolve any conflicts that come my way through effective management of my thinking. *I take control of my thoughts to minimize my experiences of uncomfortable feelings.* Then I move on with my life and all its routines.

Each day, I tell myself that I can be successful at keeping my thoughts under control. I have been victorious in the past with managing my mind, and I see triumph in the future as well.

Controlling my thinking brings positive energy into my life. I discover the rewards of peacefulness and serenity through managing my mind. My path is free of any constraints when I choose my own thoughts.

Today, I am content with life because I know I can control my thinking. I plan to reaffirm my goal to successfully manage my thoughts.

Summary of Chapters 1–3

The key to healing from the emotional toll of the pandemic is to be able to release the pain from the wounds you suffered.

In chapters 1 through 3, you learned there are three factors that have made teaching in the pandemic so difficult:

1. Your body responded to the pandemic by producing hormones and neurotransmitters that affected your emotions. It is likely you experienced or are still experiencing bouts of anxiety and/or depression.

2. The tendency is to keep thinking about life and teaching "pre-pandemic." This causes your brain to produce more hormones and neurotransmitters, resulting in greater anxiety and depression.

3. The emotions that resulted from and during the pandemic also continue the cycle.

To stop this cycle, you'll need to access your inner power, release pre-pandemic teaching, and form a new future.

In the next chapters, you'll learn how to forgive the betrayal of the pandemic, common misconceptions about forgiveness, and how to release the past of pre-pandemic teaching that may prevent you from letting go and moving forward.

Reflection–Chapters 1–3

Before moving to the next chapters, spend some time reflecting on what you've learned and discovering how it applies to you. This will prepare you for moving beyond your past and moving into the wonderful future awaiting you.

1. What are the recurring thoughts of the pandemic you don't want to have any more?

_____

_____

_____

_____

_____

_____

2. What recurring feelings of the pandemic do you not want to have anymore?

_____

_____

_____

_____

_____

_____

3. Out loud, speak to each one of these thoughts and feelings. Say this: "You are not going to be part of my life anymore." Note: This may seem strange and a bit uncomfortable at first, but when you identify and address the thought or feeling that has bogged you down, you become more aware of its effect on your everyday life, which helps you to make the necessary changes. You must address what you want to see changed!

_____

_____

_____

_____

_____

_____

Teachers of the Pandemic

Chapters 1–3 Affirmations

I am in full control of my emotions and thoughts.

I have the ability to direct my thoughts in any situation.

I choose to have thoughts that serve me. Negative thoughts create emotions and beliefs that are contrary to my purpose. I am always focused on my purpose. *In every situation, I can choose to have a thought that serves me or impedes me.* I choose to have thoughts that serve me.

By controlling my thoughts, I can control my reality. Directing my thoughts is easy for me.

In difficult times, I am focused on solutions. Only by thinking about solutions am I likely to find an acceptable one.

In pleasant times, I am focused on the experience. Allowing my mind to wander limits the amount of enjoyment I can experience. I will remain fully in the moment during pleasant times.

Negative emotions are signs that something needs to be corrected. *When I experience a negative emotion, I immediately focus on finding an alternative to that emotion.* This is the only time a negative emotion serves a useful purpose.

It can be challenging to control my thoughts and emotions. When my thoughts stray, I gently bring them back to the present. Life can only be lived and experienced in the moment.

Today, I keep my thoughts focused on the present. *I limit my mind's tendency to dwell on the past and wonder about the future.* I am in full control of my emotions and thoughts.

Chapter 4

Forgiving the Pandemic

Forgive the pandemic? What exactly does that mean? Think of the space in which you have lived. The different changes you've experienced, combined with your thoughts and beliefs, can make it difficult to release the grip of the pandemic. Add to that the biochemical response of your body, and it's a wonder most of us are still going.

In the next few chapters, you'll learn that your view of forgiveness can add to the ease of putting the pandemic behind you. You will explore what forgiveness is and what forgiveness isn't. And this knowledge will assist you in letting go of the painful elements of the pandemic and moving forward with your life in joy.

Forgiveness

Your emotions, thoughts, and beliefs, and the chemical nature of your body, can make it difficult to release and to forgive the pandemic. The memory of these past few years will remain imprinted on your educational career. **The key to healing is releasing the anger and resentment surrounding the pandemic.**

Even for the deepest of wounds, it's crucial to find a way to detach as much as possible from the pain. In most cases, this means to move into a state of forgiveness, in this case forgiveness of the system of unknowns that caused the wound.

Many people are resistant to forgiveness because they don't understand what forgiveness is. Before you explore what forgiveness is, let's take a look at what it isn't.

What Forgiveness Is Not

If they are ever told that they must forgive the pandemic and release the past to gain peace, most educators are likely to reply, "None of this was my fault. Why should I be the one to forgive?"

Within that reaction is the thought that forgiveness is about saying that the pandemic has had no responsibility or consequences in our lives.

Consider these important principles relating to forgiveness:

1. **Forgiveness is not about the pandemic and all the challenges it has presented.** When you forgive the experiences of pandemic, you're not saying that it has no responsibility for what happened to the education profession. The pandemic has caused pain.

    - Even if the pandemic had the ability to completely accept the responsibility for the pain caused, that doesn't take away your pain.

    - You are the one who is holding that pain, and you are the one who will need to let it go. No, it's not fair, but it is true.

- Forgiveness is completely about you. It's about your freedom, your peace, your future, and quite honestly, the future of the education profession.

2. **Forgiveness is not about staying in pandemic teaching patterns or returning to pre-pandemic teaching methods.** A major misconception about forgiveness is that you must remain with or return to the same teaching methodologies even if they are unproductive.

   - Your job is to care for yourself and those you're responsible for. You can forgive the pandemic, release the anger and emotional pain, and (hopefully) never experience this again.

3. **Forgiveness does not mean you didn't learn important lessons.**

   - Although it may be challenging, release your pain by forgiving the hard times, but remember the truth of the lessons learned. Accept what you learned and stay away from what hurt you.

4. **Forgiveness isn't about giving away your power or being weak.**

   - Making the choice to forgive is a choice to move forward. This is one of the most powerful things you can do for yourself.

Anyone can hold on to anger. Comparatively few can truly forgive. That is the topic of the next lesson.

Chapter 4, Part 1: Summary

In this lesson, you've learned the basics of what forgiveness is *not*. **It's the misunderstanding of what forgiveness is that blocks most people from attaining freedom from the deep hurts they've suffered during the pandemic.**

Before moving to the next chapter and learning what forgiveness *is*, take a few moments to anchor in what you've learned.

Teachers of the Pandemic
Journal Entry
Chapter 4, Part 1

Please answer these questions as fully as you can.

What is your biggest concern about forgiving the pandemic? To help with this, reread this chapter and think of the pandemic as an actual person instead of an event. You might even give it a name. More specifically, what pain did _____ (*what you named the pandemic*) cause to you? What can't you let go?

_____

_____

_____

_____

_____

_____

1. List all the reasons you have for not forgiving the pandemic. To help with this activity, humanize the event of the pandemic and really think about what you are unable to forgive about what the teaching profession experienced. Just write. Don't think. This activity is designed to unearth any hidden hurts.

_____

_____

_____

_____

_____

_____

What Forgiveness Is

Now that you know what forgiveness is not, it's time to look at what forgiveness *is*.

Very simply, forgiveness is *freedom*. It is freedom from having the experience or thought patterns of always being mindful of pandemic protocols on your mind. It is freedom from anger, frustration, and fear, which causes exhaustion (or at minimum, great resignation). It is the freedom to love your job again.

As difficult as forgiveness can be, forgiveness lightens the load on your mind, brings peace to your heart, and frees you to move forward into the future. *Refusing forgiveness affects all areas of your life.*

Holding on to the pain and resentment of the pandemic has had a major negative effect on all of us. Many of us have been so distracted that it has limited our ability to be fully productive. This may also have affected the joys of your life outside of school.

When you relive what happened, your body reacts as if you just experienced the pain. You feel like a victim and have difficulty accessing your inner strength.

Holding on to emotional pain weakens you. You are like the powerful elephant prevented from moving because it believes the little chain around its ankle controls its life.

Let's examine more deeply what forgiveness gives you:

1. **Forgiveness gives you the power to move into the future.** When you're hurt, no matter how badly, you can feel like you're carrying around a ball and chain. You hold it so tightly that you've forgotten how to release it. If you allow the pandemic to do so, that wound can lock you into pain and keep you from seeing the beauty in your life and your profession.

   - **When you release the pain, you unchain yourself, and then you throw away the chain and everything attached to it.**

   - **Your body responds and releases energy. This allows you to make plans for the future and opens your heart to reviving a new relationship with your teaching.**

2. **No longer allow your profession to be defined by the pandemic.** Forgiveness allows us to be the amazing, wonderful educator we are. Although we are changed, we are not defined by the pandemic. Remember, not all change has been bad.

   - **Define yourself by overcoming what happened and being more successful, happier, and fulfilled than anyone thought you could be.**

   - When you're not focusing on teaching in the pandemic, you'll find your path to happiness, the gift and talents you've forgotten, and the strength to look fear in the eye and move through it.

- The pandemic will have changed you, but when you release it, *you* choose to determine what happens to you, not someone else.

3. **When you forgive experiences that occurred in the pandemic, they no longer have control of you.**

   - Whatever you don't forgive, has control of you. Teaching in a pandemic had an interesting way of staying on your mind, occupying your thoughts, sapping your energy, perhaps determining where you went, who you saw, and even what you did.

   - Enough of that! Choose not to let the pandemic control your thoughts, your emotions, and your passion for teaching. Letting it all go demonstrates that the pandemic cannot continue to win. You control what you hold on to and what you release.

4. **You get to make the powerful choice of releasing the pain and moving into freedom.**

   - You'll no longer be caught in a victim consciousness. In too many aspects, we were held victim of the pandemic as we consciously watched. Victim consciousness has you believing you are powerless, making it difficult for you to take positive steps for the future.

- You demonstrate what a powerful person you are to let something go that many people cannot. **It takes great personal power to forgive the pandemic.**

- No longer will you be hypervigilant, fearing similar challenges. **Your true self will shine through, improving your current and future relationship with the teaching profession.**

5. **Your physical health improves.** When you forgive, there are powerful changes in the body that lead to a healthier and longer life.

- In the last few decades, biologists and medical researchers have discovered the power of the mind-body connection. They have found that holding on to emotional pain affects the body mentally, emotionally, and physically.

Forgiveness helps:

- Lower blood pressure

- Create a stronger immune system

- Improve heart health

- Decrease stress, which improves digestion, sexual response, sleep, and more

- Lower the risk of anxiety and depression

- Increase the "feel good: chemicals in your body

As you can see, forgiving the pandemic is one of the most powerful choices you can make to improve your life physically, mentally, emotionally, and spiritually. Embracing this choice brings positive changes in your relationship with the education profession.

Dr. Andrea C. Walker

Chapter 4, Part 2: Summary

Now that you know the positive effects forgiveness can have in every area of your life, the question you may be asking is, "How do I forgive the pandemic?" In the next module, you'll explore various methods that have been proven to assist in forgiveness. **The key is finding the one that works for you.**

Before moving on to the next lesson, please spend a few minutes to reflect on and anchor in what you've learned in this lesson.

Chapter 4, Reflection:

1. Think of someone who has hurt you and whom you haven't forgiven. Notice what happens to your body as you think of them and how your thoughts and emotions change. Now write about what you noticed.

   _____

   _____

   _____

   _____

   _____

   _____

2. Bring to mind someone whom you love and with whom you feel comfortable. Notice the changes these thoughts bring to your body, mind, and emotions. List what you've noticed.

   _____

   _____

   _____

   _____

   _____

   _____

3. Likewise, think of the pandemic. How has it hurt you? What haven't you forgiven? Notice what happens to your body and how your thoughts and emotions change as you ponder these things. Now write about what you noticed.

_____

_____

_____

_____

_____

_____

4. What are the things you love most about education? What made you decide to pursue this profession in the first place? Notice what happens to your body and how your thoughts and emotions change as you think of these things. Now write about what you noticed.

_____

_____

_____

_____

_____

_____

5. What do you want to achieve by forgiving the pandemic?

_____

_____

_____

_____

_____

_____

Chapter 4, Part 2, Reflection

Forgiveness benefits all areas of your life. When you forgive, your emotional and physical health will improve. You'll be able to think more clearly and move into your future with confidence and joy. Now all you need to know is how to accomplish this healing and life-giving process. That's what you'll learn in the next chapter. To prepare for what comes next, please take a few minutes right now to reflect on the following. This will prepare your subconscious mind for your next step into personal power.

Teachers of the Pandemic
Journal Entry

Chapter 4, Part 2

Allow yourself to answer the following as fully as you can.
Write what comes to you. Allow your mind to flow.

When I am no longer saddled with the pain of pandemic,
I will be able to:

_____
_____
_____
_____
_____
_____

Write out the reasons that a future without emotional pain
is better than feeling the way you do now.

_____
_____
_____
_____
_____
_____

Teachers of the Pandemic

Chapter 4 Affirmations

Forgiveness is a choice that I commit to.

I know I have the power to achieve whatever outcome I want. Once I commit to something, it is easy to accomplish. **Committing to forgiving the pandemic makes it a natural response whenever someone offends or hurts me.**

Controlling the actions of others is beyond my capacity, but I am able to choose *my* response.

I take a deep breath in the midst of an upsetting situation and think about my options. I choose to make my responses constructive and positive.

Forgiveness allows me to have a clear conscience and a life filled with less stress. Holding on to grudges is counter-productive because it eats away at my soul.

Having love at the center of my words and actions makes forgiveness a natural response to any differences I have with other people.

Today, forgiving the pandemic is a work in progress, but it is doable because I am committed to it. I believe that what-ever I set my mind to is achievable.

I forgive the pandemic.

I am able to forgive everyone who has ever hurt me. I let go of negativity from previous experiences and set myself free from the prison of grudges, pain, and anger.

I remove the bitterness from my heart and mind. Holding on to this pain is unnecessary and unproductive, and it keeps me a victim of my past. I choose to move forward into a life without it.

I notice the lightness I feel after letting go of the past. **I am able to find joy again because I forgive.**

I forgive myself, too. I get rid of the constant reminders of previous mistakes and errors. I do what I can to make up for my mistakes, I learn from them, and I move on with a lighter heart.

I acknowledge my feelings and forgive.

Today, I show forgiveness and move on from the pandemic. I stop allowing the past to control me and my present. **I let it go.** I get rid of the pain, sadness, anger, and resentment and replace it with new memories I can cherish.

Chapter 5

Recognize Your Power

Forgiving the pandemic is one of the biggest gifts you can give yourself. It may seem like a strange concept, but it is overwhelmingly beneficial. Forgiveness strengthens your health and brings you peace in mind and in spirit.

You've learned why forgiveness is difficult. But you can do this! You have everything you need within you to discover how you can release the pain and forgive the pandemic. You are more powerful than you ever thought you were. All you need to do is access that power and bring it forward.

**You Have the Opportunity to
Access Your Inner Power.**

The power you truly have has nothing to do with how powerful you feel. Even those you believe have accomplished much in their lives may not feel powerful. Look at everything those people in our profession accomplished during the pandemic. Amazingly, mixed feelings exist surrounding the power we exuded during this time.

**You feel powerful when you have
control over your inner world.**

1. When you control your thoughts, you control your emotions and how you respond to life.

2. When you control your emotions, you control your thoughts and your response to the difficulties of life.

3. When you control the way you respond, you control your thoughts and your feelings about the situation.

4. **When you control your thoughts, your feelings, and your response, you are able to keep the situation from becoming worse.**

During the pandemic, many of us felt as if we did not have inner control and that lent to a tendency for us to say and do things we regret. Learn from those experiences. As you work through the exercises in the chapters that follow, you'll learn how to control your thoughts, feelings, and responses by accessing the amazing power you have within you.

These concepts are key. Keep reading them until you can repeat them without hesitation.

1. **Whatever happened during the pandemic does not diminish who I am as a professional.** You still have the same talents and abilities, and perhaps even more than you had before the pandemic. These challenges might have helped you to discover how amazing you are.

    - In releasing the pandemic, you will feel more "you" than you've ever felt. When your inner vision isn't distorted by the pandemic, you can discover your gifts, talents, and inner resources.

2. **I am the most important person.** By the nature of our profession, education almost engrains us to put others before ourselves. Your well-being, inner peace, and health are all that's important in this process. Focus on yourself and what you need to do to achieve peace.

   - It's fair to assume that you might be concerned about students or other colleagues, but put them aside as you work through the following exercises.

   - **When you release pain from the pandemic, you will have the strength and energy to handle whatever is awaiting you.**

3. **What I do and say about myself is important.**

   - Remember who is most important right now: YOU. Don't allow what others say to you or about you distract you from what's important. What they're saying is not important, at least not for now.

4. **Releasing the pandemic may not be easy, but I can do it.** Whether you're building a skyscraper or releasing the pain of the pandemic, all are accomplished the same way . . . step by step.

- Although you know your ultimate goal, focus on each step, and the rest will fall into place.

5. **I am redefining myself.**

- When the pain of pandemic has been with you a long time, you may subconsciously define yourself by it. Be willing to release not only the pandemic, but also the way the pandemic has defined you.

- No matter what happened, you can be happy again. No matter what happened, you can be successful again. No matter what happened, you can have loving and fulfilling relationship with your profession again. Yes, life will be different, but it isn't over.

Chapter 5: Summary

You have within you the power and ability to achieve your desire to release the pandemic. Make a commitment to yourself to complete these exercises. The rest will fall into place.

Before moving to the next chapter, where you'll begin focusing your mind on letting go, take a few minutes to review and reflect on what you've learned about your power.

Chapter 5 Reflection

Recognizing your power benefits all areas of your life. Your emotional and physical health will improve. You'll be able to think more clearly and move into the future with confidence and joy.

Now all you need to know is how to accomplish this healing and life-giving process. That's what you'll learn in the next few chapters.

To prepare for what comes next, please take a few minutes right now to reflect on the following. This will prepare your subconscious mind for your next step into personal power.

Teachers of the Pandemic
Journal Entry

Chapter 5

The following questions are designed to assist you in incorporating what you've learned in this lesson. Describe how you want to experience your inner power.

1. Why is it crucial for you to focus on yourself as you do the exercises?

_____

_____

_____

_____

_____

_____

2. How has the pandemic defined who you are? How do you want that to change?

_____

_____

_____

_____

_____

_____

Teachers of the Pandemic

Chapter 5 Affirmations

I train my mind.

I control my feelings, thoughts, and actions. I train my mind to stay strong and healthy.

I focus on the positive. I count my blessings and express my gratitude. When faced with challenges and changes, I remind myself of what I have to gain. When I run into setbacks and delays, I find something to laugh about in the situation.

I monitor my self-talk. **I reframe my doubts and fears.** I give myself credit for making an effort. I accept myself for who I am now.

I adopt healthy habits. I work at making constructive choices automatic.

I engage in activities that sharpen my mental skills. I study foreign languages and play word games with my children. I register for online courses and shake up my daily routines.

I take care of my body. **My physical well-being affects my mental strength.** I eat nourishing whole foods, exercise regularly, and go to bed on time.

I stay connected. Spending time with family and friends reduces my stress. I learn by listening to others and sharing my opinions and experiences.

I live mindfully. **I help my brain to function effectively by organizing my schedule and minimizing distractions.** I use meditation and prayer to help me concentrate on the present moment.

Today, I give my mind a workout. I maintain a positive outlook and cultivate the kind of thoughts and behaviors that help me to succeed.

My past is behind me.

I am free of my past. What has happened no longer influences my life. I can leave the past behind me and look ahead to the future.

I use my past successes to my advantage. If I am going to look to my past, I focus on my successes. This keeps my outlook positive and hopeful.

I maintain my strongest focus on the present. I live each day to the fullest and enjoy everything that life has to offer. Many exciting things are happening around me. I steal from my present and my future when I focus on the past.

I know that I am unable to change the past. People have acted poorly toward me. I have made poor choices. However, I am still optimistic about the future.

The future can be whatever I choose to make it.

Today, I am giving up the past for the present. My mind is rooted in the present moment with an eye looking toward the future. I have a bright future, and I choose to forget the past. My life is looking better than ever.

Chapter 6

Align Your Beliefs

You learned in the last chapter that you have the personal power to release your emotional pain through forgiveness. All you need to do is follow the exercises. Take them one step at a time.

In this chapter, you'll begin your journey by aligning your beliefs to your goal of releasing all you have endured during the pandemic. You'll do this by giving direct messages to your subconscious mind. This will lay the foundation for the exercises that follow.

Give Your Subconscious Mind Directions

You may not know it, but your subconscious mind runs your life. You know those things you do automatically. That's your subconscious mind at work, making your life easier, or sometimes, harder.

Your subconscious mind can also make life difficult when it's working with outdated information. That information was great when you were a child. It might have been exactly what you wanted last week, but this week, this year even, as we move out of the pandemic, you will explore something different.

You can upgrade the data in your subconscious mind easily by telling it the following:

1. How you want your life to look

2. What you want to hear from others and yourself

3. The types of feelings you want to have

4. What smells you want

5. What you want to taste

**Upgrading the Beliefs in
Your Subconscious Mind**

Just like computer software performs upgrades for a particular program, you will upgrade your specific beliefs.

You're going to be "installing" within your subconscious mind the beliefs (the "software") you need to achieve your goal of eliminating the pain of the pandemic from your life.

There are two steps to upgrading your beliefs. The first step is identifying the beliefs you want to change. The second step is deciding what beliefs you want to place within your subconscious mind.

In chapter 1, you explored why it's difficult to release the pain from the past. This difficulty may be due to your thoughts and feelings based upon your beliefs about forgiveness. It's important to identify these old beliefs.

Examples of old beliefs to upgrade:

- **I don't have to forgive the pandemic.**

- **I don't deserve to forgive myself.**

Determine Your New Belief

Identify the new belief you want as your upgrade. Your new belief is a variation of the opposite of the old belief.

Using the old beliefs above, you'll want to upgrade to these:

- I forgive the pandemic so I'll have inner peace.

- Forgiveness allows me to have control over my life.

- When I forgive the pandemic, it stays out of my thoughts.

- I deserve to have the peace that comes from releasing the pandemic.

You might notice these new beliefs resemble affirmations that are included at the end of each chapter. Use the process below to install these affirmations into your subconscious mind.

Install Your New Beliefs

Your subconscious mind only understands concrete information. If you use abstract words such as *forgive* and *love*, your subconscious mind needs cues from your five senses to tell it what you mean.

Let's go through the process step by step.

1. **Write down the belief you want.** For this example, we'll use "I forgive the pandemic so I'll have

inner peace." Both *forgive* and *inner peace* are abstract concepts.

- **Write out two things you'll see in your life when forgiveness brings inner peace.** This needs to be something you'll see as if you were watching a video or looking at a photo.

- Perhaps inner peace means you can now go to a restaurant you've avoided because you didn't want to endanger yourself or others. You'd write out in sensory detail what going to the restaurant looks like.

- "We're at Mario's Pizza. (*sight*) I can smell pizza cooking in the oven. (*smell*) My mouth waters. (*tactile*) My friends and I are laughing. (*sound*) The pizza is hot and spicy just the way I like it. (*taste and touch*) Everyone here is smiling and eating. (*sight*)"

2. What will you overhear people saying about you when this belief is active in your life?

   The comments are about what people notice about you now that you're at peace. These could include:

   - "I haven't seen her looking this relaxed in ages!"

   - "Look at that smile on his face!"

3. What will you say about yourself?

   These comments could include:

   - "It's great to be able to have fun again!"

4. What are you feeling? This will be an emotion that is abstract. You'll give concrete examples, giving your subconscious mind a way to identify the emotion. First identify the feeling. We'll use the example of "happy":

   - Think of a time when you last felt that emotion. *When I hit a home run.*

   - Where did you feel it in your body? *In my heart.*

   - What color is the feeling? *Yellow.*

   - If happy were a shape, what would it be? *A circle.*

   - What's its texture? *Soft and smooth.*

   - What does it smell like? *Ocean candles.*

   - What does it taste like? *Peppermint candy.*

   - What's its temperature? *Warm.*

The Secret That Few People Know

For this exercise, we are going to use a mixture of learning modalities that are commonly used with our students (auditory, visual, written, and kinesthetic). Say the belief to yourself (auditory), and while speaking it, tap on your forehead three times, then your heart three times (kinesthetic). To enforce your new belief, find a picture that represents your new mindset (visual). Caption your picture with your new belief (written) and recite it daily.

These activities "awaken" your brain and create clear pathways in your heart to recognize the belief and store it in your subconscious mind.

Summary

Now that you know how to install new beliefs in your subconscious mind, fill out the next pages for each belief listed. Remember to use the four learning modalities listed above. After these beliefs are installed, move on to the next chapter to learn how to change the way you think.

Teachers of the Pandemic
Journal Entry

Chapter 6

1. I achieve peace when I forgive the pandemic.

_____
_____
_____
_____
_____
_____

2. I am in control of my life.

_____
_____
_____
_____
_____
_____

3. Forgiveness releases my emotional pain.

_____
_____
_____
_____
_____

4. I deserve to forgive myself.

_____
_____
_____
_____
_____

5. I have the energy to live a new life.

_____

_____

_____

_____

_____

_____

Dr. Andrea C. Walker

Chapter 7

Think Your Way to Freedom

Now that you've installed beliefs in your subconscious mind on forgiving and releasing the pain of your past, it's time to put those beliefs to work for you.

The next two chapters address the two major contributors to your pain: your thoughts and emotions. In this chapter you'll learn strategies to control your thoughts, as well as a powerful "trick" to command your mind to think what you want it to think.

Your Conscious Mind Can Be an Unruly Child

Your conscious mind is easily distracted. You have the power to get your mind to "sit down and be still." Although your subconscious mind is set with the new beliefs, it's time to train it in using those beliefs for your benefit.

It's time for the real *you* to take control of the unruly part of you, which enjoys running amok and causing chaos.

Try these tricks and techniques to get your conscious mind and your thoughts under control:

1. **The trick of being two different people.** This is like having two parts of yourself battling for

control. **You want your healthy self to win.** Here is an example:

- Stand tall in front of the mirror. This is your strong and powerful self, who knows that you can release the pain of the pandemic. Look yourself in the eye. The strong you is looking at the you who's in pain, overwhelmed, and tired.

- In a strong, commanding voice, say, **"It's over. It happened in the past. I cannot change the pandemic. It's time to move on."** Of course, adapt these words to suit you and your own thoughts and feelings.

- You might hear or feel a whiny little voice start to say, *But, I….* Interrupt the voice and say in a strong voice, **"No, I don't want to hear it. We have a life to live. Now, let it go!"**

- When you command your other self out loud, you're reinforcing the beliefs you installed in your subconscious mind. You're telling your subconscious mind, "Yes, I really mean that I am ready to release the pandemic and move into a healthy future."

2. **Put all your thoughts and pain in a letter…then burn it!** Research shows that writing things out with pen and paper has a positive effect upon the brain.

- **Pull out pen and paper and write a letter you won't be sending.** No one will see this except you, so don't worry about how it looks or if you are spelling everything correctly.

- Write a letter to the pandemic.

- **Put all your feelings into that letter.** Use whatever language you want. Make it as strong as you can. Put the letter somewhere safe for a day.

- A day later, pull the same letter out. As you read it, cross out words and make them even stronger. Let all your anger, frustration, and pain come out in that letter.

- Put it aside for another day.

- A day later, take the letter out again. Read it one more time. When finished, say aloud, **"I release and let it go. You have no more power over me. Be gone."** Then burn it.

- This process engages both your conscious and your subconscious mind. Give it a try. Put aside your doubts about whether or not it will work.

3. **Change your thoughts. Reliving painful events only reinjures you.** Have your strong, powerful self, the self who wants to be free of the pandemic, talk sternly but lovingly to the educator within you who is hurting.

- Say, "Stop it! We're not going there." Then say, "Remember, this is where we're going." Begin imagining, in all the sensory details, one of those wonderful images you used earlier when installing your beliefs.

- Avoid the temptation to be frustrated when you "catch" yourself rehashing the past. You'll catch yourself earlier each time until you rarely need to speak sternly to yourself.

Avoid Allowing Others to Bring You Down

Friends and family may say or do things they believe are supportive, but they may not realize they're triggering the memories and feelings you're ready to release. When that happens, it's time to take firm but loving action.

If it's appropriate, tell the person who's making the comments, "Thank you for your continued support. If you would, I'd appreciate you supporting me by not bringing it up again. Let's just talk about how wonderful life is now."

If their comments trigger negative feelings, give yourself a pep talk: "Shake it off. You're doing great. Let's go over again what life will be like when the pandemic is over." Then review one of the images you used when installing the beliefs or develop a new one.

Always remember how amazing you are and that you can release the pain of teaching in the pandemic and move to a happier professional future.

Summary

Congratulations on learning strategies on how to talk to yourself and change the way you think!

In the next chapter, you'll learn how to change the feelings that bring you down.

Before you go on to the next lesson, please take a few minutes now to reflect and anchor in what you've learned.

Teachers of the Pandemic
Journal Entry

Chapter 7

It's time for action. Please do the following now.

Write out the words you're going to use to tell your hurting self that it's time to move on to a better day and a better life.

_____

_____

_____

_____

_____

_____

Now, go to your mirror and speak aloud what you wrote. Write down what you experience.

_____

_____

_____

_____

_____

_____

Teachers of the Pandemic

Chapter 7 Affirmations

I have the power to change my thoughts.

My thoughts are under my direct control. When my thoughts are displeasing to me, I take control of the situation and redirect them. **I strive to maintain thoughts that are both helpful and pleasing to me.** I can choose thoughts that serve me.

Everyone has the power to change their thoughts. I am developing this skill and getting better at it each day.

When I control my thoughts, I control my mood and my actions. The thoughts I permit to exist ultimately determine my results. I consciously choose what I want to think about. My ability to do this is growing by leaps and bounds.

When my thoughts are distracting, disruptive, or ineffective, I take control of the situation. **I consider which thoughts would be most beneficial and change the direction of my thinking.**

Once I choose a new thought, I can maintain it with minimal difficulty. My mind is strong and capable.

My thoughts can alter my circumstances. I can alter my life and my experience in the world by changing my thoughts. Thoughts lead to actions. Actions lead to results.

Today, I actively manage my thoughts. I only entertain thoughts that propel me forward in life. **I block negative**

thoughts from remaining in my mind. I control my thoughts and my focus. I have the power to change my thoughts in an instant.

I am always looking for new ways to better my life and myself. Fortunately, almost everything in the world responds well to positive thinking. *I attract what I put out. This is why, regardless of what happens, I keep my thoughts under control.*

Because of this commitment to myself, I regularly practice meditation. There are many ways I do this: sitting at a traffic light, waiting in line at the bank, and sometimes in a formal practice, where I sit for a while and consider my thoughts. This practice assists me in being aware of my thoughts so I can control them better.

The nature of the mind is to wander. My mind does this because it is my ally and it always scans the horizon for potential danger. However, if my mind begins to focus on less preferable thoughts, I exert control over my thinking. I direct my mind to return to the topic I choose.

I feel empowered by taking charge of my thoughts. Because my thinking is under my control, I know I can make the best out of any situation and get what I want out of life.

Today, I am grateful that I know how to control my thoughts. I am confident that my ability to do this increases with time and practice. I commit to myself to meditate today to increase my mental control.

Chapter 8

Thoughts Produce Feelings

Now that you've learned ways to manage your thoughts, it's time to gain control of your emotions. You took the first step in the last chapter.

Thoughts Produce Emotions

Most people are surprised when they learn they can change their emotions. Sometimes it seems emotions "just appear." Emotions are triggered. You have the power and ability to tame those painful emotions. The skills you learned in the last chapter have prepared you for this lesson.

Feelings Are Important

Before you learn how to change your feelings, it's crucial to know that feelings aren't bad. **Feelings are a natural human response to what happens in life.** They are a signal of what brings joy, and they tell you where you are hurting.

For example, if you're with friends and someone brings up getting married, you could recall fondly your own marriage, or you could feel sadness because you're not married but would like to be.

What may be happy to one person may remind you of someone or something painful. Knowing how to work with your feelings when this happens is empowering. **These feelings aren't bad; they're painful.**

The Role of Grief

Whenever you experience a loss, you move through the stages of grief. The loss could range from scuffing your new shoes to living and teaching in a pandemic. The stages of grief are the same for both but more intense for the more painful and life-changing event.

When you scuff your shoes, you'll go through the stages quickly and, probably, only once. *Living in a pandemic, however, you will go back and forth through the various stages of grief with changes in the type and intensity of your feelings.* This includes the mishmash of feelings we discussed in the introduction.

The more deeply you've been hurt, the longer it takes to navigate the stages of grief. Be patient with yourself as you use the tools below to navigate through these feelings.

Take Care of Your Long-Term Health

When you are in the midst of the pain of grief, it's difficult to think about the consequences of your feelings on your physical, mental, and emotional health.

It's crucial for your long-term emotional and physical health to feel, work through, and release the feelings that come from grief. In the case of the pandemic, or the ending of the world's relationship with normalcy, it takes time to navigate those feelings.

For your emotional, mental, and physical health, it's important to release the anger, anxiety, and despair that can accompany the losses the pandemic inflicted. The sooner you're able to do this, the more quickly you will move on to your new future.

Adapting What You've Learned to Release Destructive Feelings

Discover how to adapt what you learned in managing your thoughts to learning how to change your feelings:

1. **The Mirror.** As we emerge from the pandemic, it's important to encourage and support yourself. **As you stand in front of the mirror, looking yourself in the eye, say aloud to yourself:**

    - "Yes, teaching in the pandemic is hard, but you will make it through this."

    - "Yes, (whatever you need to say about the pandemic), but you will make it through this."

    - **After about a month or so, change your messages to:**

    - "It's over. Let it go and move on."

    - "It's not worth staying stuck. Let's get moving."

    - When you do this, you are telling your subconscious mind, "Yes, I recognize this is difficult, but I know it'll get better."

2. **Put all your feelings in a letter . . . Then burn it.**

- Use the same process you used in releasing your thoughts. This time, focus on your feelings.

- When you're ready to burn the letter, say, **"I release this situation and all my associated feelings. I'm beginning a new life!"**

- Remember to write the letter in longhand and not type it on a computer. Writing things out in longhand is an excellent way to get those feelings out.

3. **Change your feelings.** It doesn't matter where your feelings come from; you can change them. Learning to change your feelings requires some advanced preparation.

- Recall at least three wonderful memories.

- Write each one out in detail using all five senses. Get in touch with the feelings you had at that event.

- When you catch yourself feeling miserable, tell yourself, "Nope, I'm not going to waste this time on feelings that make me miserable."

- Immediately recall one of those three happy memories. Immerse yourself in that memory until the negative feeling is gone.

- Because of the way the brain works, focusing on the happy and wonderful feeling will cancel out the unhappy one. **The more you do this, the more your brain will be trained to focus on the positive.**

Summary

As you learned how to change your feelings, you may have noticed that the exercises were similar to the ones for changing your thoughts. **Thoughts produce feelings.**

In the next chapter, you'll learn how to change your behavior so you can release the past and move into the future.

Before you move on to the next lesson, please take time now to complete the following exercise to anchor in what you've learned.

Teachers of the Pandemic
Journal Entry

Chapter 8

Take the time now to write out the wonderful memories you'll use to knock out the painful memories. Put in as much sensory detail as possible. Include:

- How it looked (colors, shapes)

- How it sounded (voices, music, other people's comments)

- How it felt (your own feelings and how your body felt)

- How it smelled (odors are a powerful trigger)

- How it tasted (foods, drink)

Describe an event in which you were proud.

_____

_____

_____

_____

_____

_____

Describe an event in which you were excited.

_____

_____

_____

_____

_____

_____

Describe an event in which you were peaceful.

_____

_____

_____

_____

_____

_____

Teachers of the Pandemic

Chapter 8 Affirmations

I channel my emotions toward positive choices.

I embrace my emotions because they connect me to my true inner self. They help me honestly express how I feel. My feelings are an integral part of me.

Even when what I am going through generates negative feelings, I use my emotions constructively. It is easy for me to find solutions to issues when I am emotionally charged up.

Sometimes taking a moment to confront my emotional state is what I need to do. Giving myself that chance helps me turn any negativity into a learning experience. When I view my feelings that way, I am able to make sound choices.

Today, I take hold of each of my emotions because they help to complete me. I am committed to using them to build a healthy and positive existence. My decisions in life are based on acknowledging and respecting my true self.

I set myself free when I release emotional burdens.

There is so much to be said for freeing myself from things that weigh me down. *When I release emotional burdens, I feel like an uncaged bird.*

Emotional burdens come when I remain in situations that break me instead of build me up. Although I sometimes feel the urge to keep going, I recognize the impact on my well-being.

Remaining in a toxic situation affects my happiness and health. There is great value in deciding to draw a line for the sake of my own physical and emotional wellness.

Negative energy dulls my spirit and moves me away from a great existence.

Saying good-bye to uncreative time wasters does my body, mind, and soul good. There is now more space to make a positive impact on the world. When I focus on positive things like spirituality and physical wellness, I feel more accomplished. There is power in letting go.

I embrace the opportunities to be happy and at peace. Those are the times when I can live my best life.

Today, I vow to release myself of each thing that is weighing me down emotionally. My days are well spent when I make room for healthy energy. There is beauty in giving myself the space to grow in a meaningful and positive way.

Chapter 9

Changing Behavior

By reading the lessons and doing the exercises, you gain strategies to change the thoughts and feelings that resulted from holding on to the pain of the pandemic.

The last area to be aware of is your own behavior. Repetitive actions become habits. Habits are actions that occur without thought. Recovery from the pandemic requires that you apply thought to your actions and behaviors.

Know the Definition of Insanity

If you want to buy a vegetarian meal but you always go to the steakhouse that puts bacon in its vegetables, you're never going to get a vegetarian meal. Every time you go to that restaurant wanting a vegetarian meal, you will be disappointed. That is an example of "insanity."

Insanity is repeatedly doing the same thing, expecting different results.

If you continue to operate your school or classroom the same way you did prior to the pandemic, and you leave the classroom feeling down or angry each time, you're the living example of insanity. True, you may feel like you're going insane with everything you're carrying, but there's no reason to make it worse.

To recover from teaching in the pandemic, it's time to embrace the challenge of finding new things to do, new places to go, and new ways of doing things.

From Insanity to Victimization

Many people are walking examples of the definition of *insanity*. They also begin to feel like victims, because nothing is working out for them. You may have felt like a victim when the pandemic began, **but you no longer need to remain a victim in the profession you love!**

When everything pertaining to the pandemic is over, we will be left with a major challenge. That challenge is pulling ourselves out of feeling like victims and getting back in touch with the amazing, powerful educators who are hiding beneath the weight of the pandemic.

You are the only one who can pull yourself out of repetitive and nonproductive behaviors and become the wonderful you!

Behaviors Can Trigger Thoughts and Emotions

Your actions can assist in your goal to release the pandemic or they can hold the past firmly in place. It's crucial to be aware of what behaviors are triggering your emotional pain. **Once you know your triggers, stay away from them!** That may be more difficult than you think, but you can do it.

Find New Things to Talk About

Avoid talking about teaching in the pandemic with almost everyone. Talking about what happened just brings up the negative feelings. Confine your discussion about "the pandemic" to sessions with a therapist, a coach, a spiritual leader, or a support group.

Best friends, family members, and those who enjoy hearing gossip may not help you. Your friends and family may want to give advice and support, but talking with them may keep the pain going.

Someone objective better assists in moving past the pain. An objective outsider can point out why or where you're continuing to hurt yourself and how to stop.

If you still have the need to "talk," use the releasing exercise—working on writing the same letter three times and then burning it. Repeat that process as often as needed.

Go to New Places

The pandemic confined many of us to our homes and slowly put routines of isolation into place. Getting back to "normalcy" means getting back to a more active lifestyle. Get out and do new things and experience new places. For instance, if you always went to Joe's Pizza for dinner during the pandemic, it's time to get acquainted with Penelope's Pizza. If you always ordered pepperoni and pineapple pizza, it's time to order a different kind. Better yet, go to a cooking class and learn to make something new and different for yourself!

You may wonder why you need to consider changing the places you go. Have you ever heard the phrase, "Familiarity breeds contempt"? Basically, the close associations to familiar pandemic routines may have somehow caused you pain—or they could bring back that pain. Certain places may trigger unpleasant feelings and unconsciously keep you in a pandemic mindset. You don't need to change anything if it does not resurrect the pain of the pandemic. Pay attention to your body's feelings and the attached associations when doing familiar routines. If being in a certain place continues to hurt you, **quit doing what hurts.**

Music Is a Powerful Memory Trigger

Music is also a powerful trigger. The memories associated with it can resurrect the experience of loss quickly. This is true for any music. Find new songs to enjoy about life as the pandemic ends.

Quit Attempting to Figure Out What Went Wrong Unless You're with a Therapist

It's natural to want to know what you could have done differently. To discover what went wrong, you often need a therapist or some type of life coach.

Just remember that you can't change the past, but you can apply your new knowledge to change your future and professional life.

Summary

Congratulations on almost finishing this book!

You've learned what happens in your brain when you're hurt emotionally. You've also learned why forgiveness, or letting go, is so important.

You now have powerful tools and tips to change your thoughts and emotions so you can release the pain of the pandemic as quickly as possible. And you learned in this lesson the importance of changing certain behaviors, so those thoughts and emotions aren't triggered.

Before you celebrate the completion of this book and your new outlook, take a few minutes to answer these reflection questions so you can anchor in what you've learned.

Teachers of the Pandemic
Journal Entry

Chapter 9

Please write out your answers to the following questions.

What activities result in painful pandemic memories or have strong associations to the pandemic for you?

_____
_____
_____
_____
_____
_____

What can you do instead of participating in these activities?

_____
_____
_____
_____
_____
_____

What qualities are you ready to find again? List as many as you can.

_____
_____
_____
_____
_____
_____

Teachers of the Pandemic

Chapter 9 Affirmations

I am free to create my own reality.

I am in control of my destiny. I am responsible for my life. I avoid blaming others for challenges. **I avoid blaming circumstances for the direction my life has taken.** I choose the path for my life with my own day-to-day choices.

I believe that my life is what I make it.

My version of reality exists within me. While others may have a view of life filled with fear and limits, my reality is different. **My reality consists of limitless opportunities.** I am in awe of the possibilities that exist for my life. I make a conscious effort to hold a perspective that provides me with as many options as possible.

I create a positive reality for my life by freeing my mind of hate, fear, and jealousy. I make room in my mind for positive thoughts and emotions. **Holding negative energy ensures that my reality will be unpleasant.** I release any negative energy and focus on the positive.

I accept the changes that naturally occur in life. Resistance is a waste of time and energy. I allow reality to be reality. **What I can change are the perceptions and beliefs I hold in my mind.** The external world is largely outside of my control. This is fine, because my beliefs and focus are what determine my reality.

Today, I am making my strongest effort to create a reality that serves my life's purposes. I have the hope and ambition necessary to make positive changes in my life. I am free to create my own reality.

Chapter 10

Final Exam

Congratulations! You have learned the tools and strategies that will assist you in changing the thoughts, feelings, and behaviors that anchor you in the past. You now know that you can manage those three things when you access your personal power.

As you use the strategies you have learned, you'll find the pain of the pandemic lessening. Your mind will clear, and you will be able to focus on what's important to you. You'll begin to move into your new future!

Reflection

**Describe what you would do
in the following situations:**

You're asked to cover for a colleague who is absent on the only free hour you have for the day due to a lack of substitutes. (Remember, this question is for all educational personnel, not just teachers. To make schools operate, all members of the school staff have had to contribute when others are absent.)

Your gut clenches, and you are immediately overwhelmed. What can you do immediately, and what can you do later?

_____
_____
_____
_____
_____
_____

You're on social media when you see someone speaking in negative terms about you, your team, or your school or school district in general. The old hurt comes roaring back. What can you do to release the pain? You can't quit thinking about what happened. What can you do?

_____
_____
_____
_____
_____
_____

Boundaries are a highly underrated topic. And yet the need to be implemented to keep the positive in and the negative out of your life. What boundaries do you need to construct whenever you feel sad? What can you do to put these boundaries in place?

_____
_____
_____
_____
_____
_____

Teachers of the Pandemic

Chapter 10 Affirmations

I avoid self-pity.

I accept my life the way it is. When things go wrong, I stay strong. I avoid dissolving into a puddle of tears or feeling sorry for myself. I avoid anxiety and additional stress.

I understand that I am responsible for my actions.

When I make a mistake, I accept the responsibility and the consequences. I do what I can to correct the situation or make amends, I learn what I can from the error, and then I move on without worrying further about it.

I am in control of my emotions.

I reject the idea that I am a victim. I avoid negative thoughts and feelings and focus on the positive aspects of any situation.

When I encounter a challenge, I remind myself that such obstacles are a normal part of life, and I get busy seeking a solution. I know that I am a strong individual who is capable of overcoming obstacles.

I accept my circumstances—whatever they may be.
Letting go sets me free.

Holding on to the past undermines my happiness and productivity. *Letting go frees me and allows me to achieve my highest potential.*

I accept that everything changes. When change occurs, I adjust my expectations and realize that relying on temporary conditions for security is pointless.

I remove the conditions I have been placing on my happiness.

I recognize that some events are beyond my control, and I accept that letting go is the best option. There are times when I lose sight of what I value. But if I wait until the decision is out of my hands, I will pay a higher price. By anticipating natural shifts, I make the inevitable adjustment easier.

I transform my intentions regarding my relationships with others. I care more about their welfare than how they make me feel.

I examine my thoughts and let go of those that are holding me back. I realize it is more constructive to manage whatever circumstances arise than to waste time wishing my life was different.

Letting go is an ongoing process. Starting with small issues trains me to handle bigger challenges. Showing myself that I can survive without cable TV might inspire me to ride my bike to work instead of driving.

My heart is more open to new opportunities when I let go. My future appears brighter.

Today I am more determined than ever to be more flexible. I am ready to let go of teaching in the pandemic and start over.

Teachers of the Pandemic Quiz

Chapter 10

Choose the correct answer.

1. You don't always know how powerful you are.

    A. True

    B. False

2. Who is most important in the process of forgiving?

    A. The others involved

    B. You

    C. Your friends

    D. Your family members

3. When you release the past and forgive, you'll:

    A. Redefine yourself

    B. Tap into your inner power

    C. Keep the situation from getting worse

    D. All the above

4. Sometimes you need to tell loved ones how to support you as you're healing from the pain of the past.

    A. True

    B. False

5. Looking in the mirror and commanding yourself to "get over it":

    A. Proves you have a split personality

    B. Reinforces the belief that you can and will release the past

    C. Is a sign you're crazy

    D. Convinces you it's time for ice cream

6. Controlling your thoughts will prevent you from reinforcing the pain of the past.

    A. True

    B. False

7. You can change your feelings by:

    A. Remembering times when you felt proud of yourself

    B. Crying in your favorite pizza place

    C. Listening to your favorite song over and over and over

    D. Hitting yourself on the head with a rubber hose

8. You can change your behavior by:

    A. Doing new things

    B. Finding new favorite places to go

    C. Discovering new music you enjoy

    D. All the above

9. Whether you know it or not, you have the personal power to release the past and move into a wonderful future.

    A. True

    B. False

10. The following will help you to forgive and release the past:

    A. Your inner strength

    B. Your determination to be happy

    C. Completing the exercises in the lessons

    D. All of the above

Answer Key

1. A

2. B

3. D

4. A

5. B

6. A

7. A

8. D

9. A

10. D

Dr. Andrea C. Walker

Author * Speaker * Coach

Find out more about Dr. Walker

Official Website
www.theredtomatoes.com

Halo Website
https://halopublishing.com/dr-andrea-c-walker/

Instagram
www.instagram.com/theredtomatoes